The Story of Noah's Ark

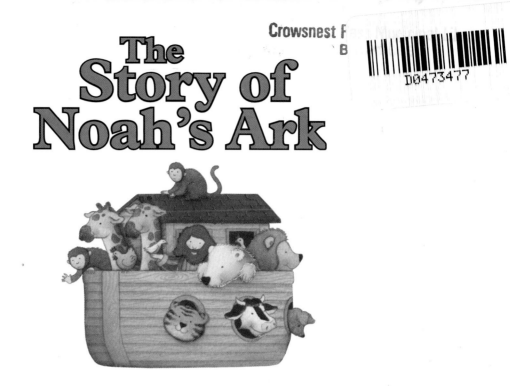

retold by **Allia Zobel-Nolan**

illustrated by **Trace Moroney**

This book belongs to

_____

This is the story from Genesis, chapters 6 to 9, of Noah,
the animals, and the big flood. It teaches us to trust
God will protect us and keep us safe.

retold by Allia Zobel-Nolan
illustrated by Trace Moroney
Published by Reader's Digest Children's Books
Reader's Digest Road, Pleasantville, NY U.S.A. 10570-7000 and
Reader's Digest Children's Publishing Limited,
The Ice House, 124-126 Walcot Street, Bath UK BA1 5BG
Manufactured in China.
10 9 8 7 6 5 4 3 2 1

God told Noah, "Build a big boat."
Then God told Noah to bring two of every animal and
his entire family aboard.

Genesis 6:7

In the beginning, when God created the world, it was a beautiful place. Then, little by little, most people forgot about God. They did bad things and were not nice to each other. This made God sad. But there was one man who still loved God. His name was Noah. So God spoke to

Noah and told him his plan. "I'm starting over," God said. "I'm sending rain to cover the earth. It will wash away everything. But don't worry, I'll keep you safe," God said. "I promise."

Afterward, God told Noah to build a boat—not just any boat, but a special one made out of cyprus, called an ark. And God was very specific. "Make it 450 feet long," he said, "75 feet wide, and 45 feet high. Give it an upper, middle, and lower deck," he continued, "and cover it inside and out with tar."

Noah listened first, then started right away. He sent for his three sons, Shem, Ham, and Japeth, and they all got to work. They sawed wood, and they hammered in nails. They made rooms, and windows, and a great big door for the boat. Then God told Noah about the animals.

"I'm sending you animals," God said. "Birds that fly, bugs that crawl, giraffes with long necks, and elephants with big noses. I'm sending polar bears, and lions, and all manner of living creatures," God said. "Take two of each on board,"

God continued. Then God told Noah about the food. "Gather some of every kind and bring it with you. You're going to need it."

Drip, drop, drip, drop, drip, drop. God sent the rain. It came down softly, but steadily. As it did, Noah's family made themselves at home on the ark. Then Noah went to check up on the animals. "Don't worry," Noah told them.

"Everything will be okay. God has promised to protect us. He'll keep us safe." *Purr*, went the tiger as he nestled in Noah's lap.

The rain continued. It fell faster and faster. Suddenly, without a word—BAM—God shut the door. And still the rain poured down. Puddles grew, and the water rose higher and higher.

Noah, his family, and the animals waited. Soon the water covered the grass, the flowers, and even the trees. Then, all at once, the great big boat started to move. "Hold on," Noah said. "Here we go."

Soon, lightning was flashing and—KABOOM—thunder roared. The ark rocked back and forth on the sea of rain. But God kept his promise. Noah and the animals were safe and sound.

The ark Noah had built was warm and dry, and there was plenty of food to eat. "When will the rain stop?" Noah's wife asked him. "When God wants it to," Noah replied.

Forty days came and went. Then one day, the sun began to shine. Noah went up on deck. Whales were playing tag and a strong wind was blowing. "The water will dry up soon," he said.

Days passed, and Noah sent a raven to look for land. The bird flew back quickly. "Nothing yet," Noah said to his wife. So they waited. Noah tried again—only this time he sent a dove.

The dove returned and flew over their heads. In its beak was a branch from an olive tree. Noah knew then that the ground was starting to dry. "Hurray," cried Noah and his family. The animals sniffed the fresh air once again and smiled. "It won't be long now," Noah said. As the water continued to dry up, he began to see the tops of mountains. So he sent the dove out again, and this time, it did not return.

Meantime, the ark had come to a full stop. Noah saw that the ground was dry. Then he heard God say, "Come out, now, Noah. Leave the ark." Noah thanked God for keeping his promise. Then he looked up in the sky.

"It's a rainbow," God said. "I put it in the sky as a sign of my love. It means I'll never flood the earth again." So Noah and his family, and all the animals went their way, enjoying the green earth once more.

Do you remember all the animals in the story?

Can you name an animal with a long neck?

Can you name an animal with a striped coat?

Can you roar like a lion?

Can you meow like a cat?

Can you wiggle your nose like a mouse?

Can you answer these questions?

1. What were Noah's sons' names?

2. Who shut the door when everyone was in the ark?

3. How many days did it rain?

4. What did the dove bring back to the ark?

5. What did God put in the sky to show his love?

Turn the page for the answers.

Answers:
1. Shem, Ham, and Japeth 2. God 3. Forty days and forty nights
4. An olive branch 5. A rainbow